Other Books In This Series Are:

Stressed Out?
Bryan Robinson, Ph.D.

Angry? Do You Mind If I Scream?
Devon Weber

I Don't Need Therapy But . . .
Laurie Weiss, M.A.

Health Communications, Inc.
3201 S.W. 15th Street
Deerfield Beach, Fl 33442-8190
Phone: (800) 851-9100

WHERE DO I DRAW THE LINE?

How To Get Past
Other People's Problems
And Start Living Your Own Life

Carla Wills-Brandon, M.A., P.A.

Health Communications, Inc.
Deerfield Beach, Florida

Carla Wills-Brandon
Houston, Texas

©1991 Carla Wills-Brandon
ISBN 1-55874-141-0

Publisher: Health Communications, Inc.
          3201 S.W. 15th Street
          Deerfield Beach, Florida 33442-8190

Introduction

———

For those of us who come from dysfunctional families, the concept of boundaries, let alone healthy boundaries, is probably incomprehensible. In my own recovery I had been abstaining from addictive acting-out behavior for several years before I even heard the word "boundary." During this time I was making cookies for the entire recovering community when asked, spending hours on the phone listening to the problems of others at the expense of taking care of myself and never, never saying *no* to requests.

I felt emotionally, physically and spiritually burned out and could not understand why I felt so miserable. After a great deal of painful investigating, I found I was not only being victimized by others with me in recovery, but also was unknowingly violating the boundaries of friends, family and peers. I felt lost and confused. In order to determine what my concept of a boundary was, I began to re-examine my childhood years, this time exploring the development — or lack of development — of my boundaries within my family of origin.

What I discovered was frightening: I didn't know what a healthy boundary was! My family system had fluctuated throughout my youth from chaotic enmeshment to controlling rigidity. Before I could begin to develop healthy boundaries, I was going to have to take an in-depth look at what I had to work with.

I went to workshop after workshop on achieving healthy boundaries but could never seem to get it. I would hear about this technique or that behavior change which would really facilitate healthy development of boundaries, but nothing seemed to stick.

I remember being at a marathon workshop on boundaries (I was really serious about this stuff) but still felt dissatisfied with what I had learned. I even asked the facilitator where in the hell I could *buy some.* I was desperate! I kept hearing a lot of theory and book definitions, but nothing I could grasp and hang on to. Slowly I discovered that my own dysfunctional boundaries were related to what I had learned growing up in my family of origin. With this personal knowledge, change began.

This Workbook Is For You

It is a tool that can help you discover not only how your family of origin upbringing created your dysfunctional boundaries, but how these same boundaries — or lack of boundaries — are working in your life today.

As you investigate this issue with the help of this workbook, you will begin to re-evaluate those tools you developed in childhood — tools that no longer work. After examining what you do have with respect to boundaries, you will be able to determine what you need to do to begin establishing healthy boundaries.

Most of us still carry the skills that worked during childhood in our dysfunctional family systems. We continue to act out these established patterns without giving them a second thought. We discover at one point or another that something is not working but have difficulty putting our finger

directly on the problem. Usually this is because we are dealing with old survival skills
learned in childhood in response to abuse,
trauma, chaos and parental dependency and
we don't have the tools we need to re-evaluate these old skills. It takes a great deal of
honesty, an open mind and commitment, but
the rewards can be immense. By acknowl-
edging your boundary difficulties, you have,
as is said in many support groups, begun to
"move from the problem into the solution!"

My best to you.
Carla Wills-Brandon

EXPLORING YOUR FAMILY OF ORIGIN

The first several questions deal with your family of origin's perceptions of privacy. Did your family fail to provide privacy for each individual family member? Or were family members so guarded and secretive that today you feel uncomfortable opening up and sharing with others in any way, shape or form?

Most of us will find our families were chaotic in some respects, extremely guarded and secretive in others. As you explore your childhood you will be able to see parallels in your adult life.

PRIVACY

1. Do you feel you were allowed privacy in your family of origin? _____ Describe how: _____
_____

2. Were you allowed privacy in your own room, or did family members walk in and out freely? _____ If you did not have privacy in your room,

how did that feel? _____

_____

3. If your parents rarely came into your room, did you feel they just weren't interested? _____

4. Did people knock before coming into your room? _____ If not, how did you feel about it? _____

_____

5. Did you feel safe in your room? _____ Why? _____

_____

6. Did you feel safe undressing in your room, or were you afraid someone would walk in unannounced while you were changing clothes? _____ If people walked in unannounced, how did you feel?_____

_____

7. Were you allowed to have a lock on your door? _____

8. If you didn't have a lock on your door, did you ever wish for one? _____ Why? _____

_____

9. When you were younger, did you suffer from any of the following?

_____ Night terrors

_____ Fear of snakes or spiders in your room

_____ Fear of something horrible under the bed

_____ Difficulty sleeping

_____ Wetting the bed past toddler years

_____ Fear of vampires, robbers or monsters getting into your room

_____ Fear of the dark

_____ Fear of getting out of bed in the middle of the night to go to the bathroom

_____ A need to cover your head with blankets or pillows for protection

_____ A need to wear extra clothing for protection

The above are symptoms of childhood sexual abuse. If you answered *yes* to several of the above, you may have some repressed abuse issues in need of exploration. If this is so, I suggest you read my book *Is It Love Or Is It Sex: Why Relationships Don't Work* for more information. Or read *You Can Overcome Childhood Abuse: Even Sexual Abuse* by Martha Baldwin. Abuse of any kind damages our boundaries.

10. Did you ever hear your parents quarrel late in the night when you were in bed? _____ If so, how did you feel about it then? _____

    _____

    How do you feel about it now?_____

    _____

11. Did either of your parents ever come into your room to complain about the other parent or to discuss problems they were experiencing in their private lives? _____ If so, how did you feel about that? _____

    _____

    If it made you feel uncomfortable, explain why: _____

    _____

    If it made you feel special, explain

how: _____

_____

If your parents never shared themselves with you, did you feel isolated, alone, abandoned, rejected or left out?

_____

_____

If not, how else did you feel? _____

YOUR SPACE

Personal space is very important for our well-being and sense of security. Having our own personal space during childhood not only teaches us how to be responsible for ourselves in adulthood but also teaches us to respect the personal space and boundaries of others. Having our own space in childhood provides a training ground to help us develop the boundary tools we need for successful adult lives.

12. Close your eyes and imagine the room or rooms you grew up in. Did you share the room with anybody else? _____ If so, did you enjoy that experience? _____ If you enjoyed

the experience, describe how it was enjoyable: _____

_____

If you didn't enjoy the experience, explain why: _____

_____

If you shared a room, did you have your own space? _____
If not, what was that like? _____

_____

If you did have your own space, how did you differentiate your space from that of the person you shared the room with? _____

_____

13. Did you have your own closet and drawer space? _____ Did you have to share your clothes with a sibling? _____ If so, how do you feel about that?_____

_____

Did people in your family borrow your things without asking? _____ If so, how do you feel about that? _____

_____

14. If your family was very rigid about using each other's property, how do you feel about that? _____

_____

Do you wish they would have shared more with one another?

_____

15. Do you share a room with somebody now? _____ If so, do you have your own closet space and drawer space? _____ If not, describe your situation:

_____

Does your spouse, lover or roommate respect your private space and ask before entering your closet or drawer space? _____ If not, how does it feel? _____

_____

Do you enter your spouse's, lover's or roommate's closet space or drawers without permission? _____ How does he or she react? _____

_____

16. Do you feel you can leave your personal belongings out in your room and still have your privacy respected? _____ If not, how do you feel about that? _____

    _____

    If you leave your wallet, purse, journal or briefcase out in the open, do you trust your privacy will be respected?_____

17. Do you ever look through other family members' closets, drawers, wallets, briefcase or purses? _____ If so, why? _____

    How do you feel about your "why" answer? _____

    _____

18. Do other family members ever refer to you as a snoop or busybody or become angry upon learning you have been in their personal belongings? _____ If so, how do you feel about their responses? _____

    _____

YOUR BED

Having our own bed in childhood also teaches us about personal space and boundaries. When my son Aaron was about three years old, he began demanding that I not lie on his bed with him at nap time. He would say proudly, "Mamma, this is my bed! You have your own bed downstairs." He was learning he had a right to his own space and was setting a boundary with me in response to his new awareness. I was surprised at how early children learn about boundaries, and how so many of us were not allowed the experiences necessary for boundary building.

19. In childhood, did you have your own bed to sleep in? _____ If not, who did you share a bed with? _____
All children need their own sleeping space and their own bed. It is abusive not to provide sleeping space for a child, but many parents take a child to bed with them, believing this is for the child's own good. In reality the child may be a buffer between

Mom and Dad, or the parent may be lonely and in need of a sleep partner. When children continually get out of their beds and sleep with their parents, this is a sign of possible childhood trauma that needs investigation. If you had to share a bed, how do you feel about that? _____

Did you ever wish for your own bed? _____

20. If you slept with a parent on a regular basis, did you ever feel special? _____ Did you ever sleep with one parent while the other parent slept elsewhere? _____ If so, did you feel more important than the parent who was not sleeping in the parental bed? _____

21. Do you remember a time in your childhood when somebody touched you on your genitals or had you touch them on their genitals while in bed? _____ If so, please describe the incident: _____

_____

How did you feel about the incident
then? _____

_____

How do you feel about it now? _____

_____

Many believe that since such experiences
happened a long time ago, they do not affect
us now. This is far from true. If you have had
such experiences and have not sought out
help in resolving the trauma of these abuses,
I strongly suggest you do so. Groups like Survivors of Incest Anonymous can be of great
value in aiding in the recovery process.

22. If you do not remember an incident
    such as the above happening to you,
    but suspect that it is a possibility,
    write out your reasoning for such
    suspicion (that is, symptoms): _____

_____

We may have many symptoms of abuse,
yet we do not retain the memories of our
abuse experiences. This is quite normal and
is the way the mind protects us until we are
ready to deal with the issues related to the
abuse. Identifying the symptoms of abuse

we carry is a good way to facilitate memories of abuse that have been repressed.

Aside from those symptoms described in question 9, there are other indicators of unresolved abuse. Check if the following apply to you in any way:

_____ Excessive memory loss from childhood

_____ Feeling at times that life doesn't have any meaning

_____ Suicidal feelings on a regular basis, attempts or threats

_____ Sexual dysfunction

_____ Phobias or phobic behavior

_____ Panic attacks, shortness of breath, light-headedness

_____ Sexual avoidance behavior or a dislike for sex

_____ Sexual addiction

_____ Dysfunctional relationships with addicted individuals

_____ Excessive fears of males, females, homosexuality, blood, shots

_____ Extreme difficulty with dentists, doctors

_____ Numbness in parts of body (hands, legs, arms and so on)

_____ Eating disorders

_____ Adolescent sexual acting-out (inappropriate behavior)

_____ Teenage pregnancy

_____ Teenage venereal disease

_____ Involvement in emotionally, physically or sexually abusive relationships in adulthood

_____ Sleep disorders in adulthood

_____ Chemical dependency issues in adolescence

_____ Chemical dependency issues in adulthood

_____ No children

_____ Recurring gastrointestinal difficulties

_____ Frequent urinary track disorders with onset in childhood

_____ Low-grade depression that rarely dissipates

_____ Frightening nightmares, many of which are repetitive

_____ Fearful fantasies that are not reality based

_____ Difficulty feeling feelings

_____ Muscle tremors and ticks

_____ Overwhelming feelings of anxiety that are difficult to explain

_____ Frightening scenes that come into your mind

_____ Overwhelming reactions to violence and/or sexual scenes on television, in the movies or in magazines and books

_____ Confusing sex with love

_____ Inability achieving healthy intimacy in relationships

_____ Confusion about own sexual identity

_____ Having relatives within the family system who have been abusive

_____ Many psychosomatic illnesses that are rarely resolved

_____ Allergies, unexplained vaginal or ure- thral discharge in childhood, abdominal pains, unexplained rashes, asthma

_____ Hair-pulling during childhood and, for some, in adulthood

_____ Self-mutilating behavior: cutting, scab-picking, self-injury

_____ Denial of physical pain

_____ Out-of-body experiences, excessive fantasy, dissociation

If you have five or more of the above, chances are you have some unresolved trauma in your life in need of resolution. Unresolved trauma continues to affect us until we give it the attention it deserves. It also affects our ability to maintain healthy boundaries and to set limits with others in adult ways.

If you recall your abuse issues from childhood, please list them below:

23. Were you ever awakened late at night to be abused, lectured or harassed, or were you ever awakened by the disruptive behavior of an alcoholic or rageaholic parent, grandparent or sibling? _____ These are boundary violations. If you answered yes, describe the incidents.

_____

Incident of Abuse	How I Felt Then*	What I Did Then	How I Feel About It Now	What I Would Do Now
The Dysfunction In Your Family Of Origin	Your History, Which Set Up Your Present-Day Dysfunctional Behavior	Where Your Dysfunctional Boundaries Originated	Your Unfinished Family Of Origin Business	Your Recovering Behavior Today

---

*_Feelings Guide:_ Names of feelings include shame, anger, terror, sadness, loneliness, hate, rage, fear, grief, abandonment, joy, security, love, protected, numb (numb is a feeling when it isn't safe to feel anything else).

YOUR ROOM

In childhood our bedrooms provide us with space in which we can begin to discover who we are, what we like and what we don't like. How we decorate our childhood and adolescent room describes who we are as individuals and provides us with opportunities to begin experimenting without concepts of self. Our rooms also provide us with a safe retreat not only from family problems, but from life in general when the world feels too overwhelming. This piece of space gives us a place to hide out when the pain that accompanies growing up becomes too much for us to not only bear but understand. If we do not have the safety of our "own place," we grow up feeling not only unsafe but lost. We don't know that we have a right to take time and space for ourselves in adulthood. Taking a look at how we felt about our own personal space in childhood can provide some of the answers to our difficulty with boundaries in adulthood.

24. Did your parents rarely check up on you in your room? _____ Do you be-

lieve you did not receive enough interested attention from your parents with regard to your activities in
your room? _____
Do you wish your parents would
have paid more attention to you and
your activities? _____ How would
you have liked them to show more
interest? _____
_____

25. Were you too free to do as you
pleased in your room? _____ If so,
how do you feel about this now?
_____

26. Were you allowed to decorate your
own room as you pleased, or did you
have guidelines? _____ If you had
guidelines, do you feel they were appropriate or too rigid? _____
Did your room express your personality or that of a parent or caretaker? _____ If it expressed your personality, describe how: _____
How do you feel about that? _____
Did you like your room? _____ Tell

why or why not: _____

_____

Did your parents take an interest in how your room was decorated by being supportive and encouraging? _____ If not, how do you feel about that? _____

_____

27. Did you have a bedtime curfew? _____ If so, do you believe it was reasonable? _____ If you didn't have a bedtime curfew, how do you feel about that? _____

_____

Children need structure in their lives. If the structure is too rigid, it can stunt creativity and the development of healthy independence. If parents do not provide healthy structure, discipline, support and guidelines, children do not develop these necessary skills for successful living in adulthood. Healthy guidelines teach us how to set limits with ourselves and others. Guidelines during childhood also provide us with a sense of security. Do you feel you received the above? _____

_____

28. Take a look at your answers to questions 1 to 27 and describe how they relate to the boundaries you have in your adult life: _____
_____
_____

    Are there any parallels? _____ Describe how your family of origin upbringing regarding your personal space in childhood has affected you today: _____
_____
_____

29. What are the problem areas you need to address for your recovery and the development of healthy boundaries?
    • _____
    • _____
    • _____

Do you promise yourself to explore these areas of difficulty? *If* you said yes, congratulations! You are on your way to repairing your damaged boundaries.

YOUR BATHROOM

Bathrooms are always an excellent gauge of a family system's boundaries. Some families are chaotic and others are rigid with respect to personal privacy. In chaotic families people use one another's toothbrushes, combs, razors and makeup without asking. In rigid families it is an unspoken rule that personal articles are never to be touched by anyone other than the owner. In families lacking in boundaries, privacy is unheard of. People walk in on one another while the toilet is in use or during bathing, seeing this as normal family behavior. In families with rigid barriers, family members are overly cautious with regard to everyday experiences, such as bathing, using the toilet, nudity and so on. The following questions will allow you to explore the rules and boundaries your family followed with regard to the bathroom. We will also examine how those childhood experiences continue to affect your boundaries today.

30. Did your family have rules and regulations for bathroom use? _____ If so, list rules (Example: Lifting toilet seat for males, shutting door during use, cleaning up after self.)

- _____
- _____
- _____
- _____
- _____

31. What is your earliest memory of the bathroom? (Bathing, toilet-training, watching a parent bathe or shave):

_____

How do you feel about this memory?

_____

_____

32. How many bathrooms do you remember having in the house or houses you grew up in? _____ Did your parents have a bathroom separate from the children? _____ If so, were you ever allowed to use their bathroom? _____ If everybody shared one bathroom, did you have a drawer or place for your bathroom articles? _____

33. What were the family rules regarding use of the toilet? (Having to shut the door, knocking to see if the bath-

room was in use.) List three specific
rules:

- _____
- _____
- _____

34. Did family members ever walk in on
you unannounced while you were using the toilet? _____ If yes, what
was your response to this and how
did you feel? _____

_____

Was this occurrence rare, regular or
often? _____

35. When my son, Aaron, turned two
and a half, he began telling Michael
and me to leave him alone when he
was using the toilet. He would also
close the door, setting a limit with
us that said he wanted to use the
toilet by himself. If your parents
wanted to come into the bathroom
and you were using it, were you able
to say no? _____ If so, what was
their response? _____

_____

If not, what was your response? ___
_____

36. Did your parents or siblings ever use the toilet in front of you? ____ How did you feel about this? _____
_____

37. I once walked into a boutique to do some shopping. I followed the owner as she carried my choice of clothes to the dressing area. She was talking with me on the way there. Then she said she needed to use the restroom. She continued talking to me as she entered the restroom — which opened onto the dressing area — and proceeded to use the toilet with the door open while I was still standing outside. I was stunned, but she continued using the toilet in my presence as if this were normal procedure. This action told me a great deal about her family of origin and their boundaries.

When a friend or relative or spouse uses the toilet in front of you today, how do you feel about this?

Does it seem normal, uncomfortable or offensive? _____

38. Do you use the toilet in front of others? _____

39. Are you overly cautious in your use of the toilet? _____ If so, how do you feel if someone accidentally walks in on you while you are using the bathroom? _____

40. In some families parents are overly concerned with fecal material and urine and have an overwhelming need for cleanliness. Some children are shamed or scolded for not wiping themselves properly or putting the toilet seat down. Did you have any of these experiences? _____ If so, describe them: _____

41. If your family was overly concerned with cleanliness, describe how that was acted out in your family system _____

Did you ever feel as though urination or defecation were nasty, ugly, shameful behaviors to be hidden and not talked about? _____

42. Shame about urination or defecation can affect us in adult life, setting us up to be fearful of germs or dirty things. Some of us can even become somewhat phobic of bathrooms in gas stations or restaurants or of our own bodily smells and excretions. Does the above relate to you at all?

_____

43. What is your earliest memory of a bathing experience in childhood? ___

_____

Is this a pleasant or unpleasant memory? _____

44. At what age did your parents stop bathing you and allow you to bathe yourself? _____ When children reach age three to four, they are very capable of bathing themselves and usually ask to do so.

45. Do you remember which parent was the most responsible for seeing to it that you were bathed? _____

46. Did you ever bathe with a sibling or parent? _____ If so, describe your experience: _____

_____

After toddler age it is sexually abusive for parents to bathe with children. Children need to be allowed personal space and privacy for bathing because it teaches them what privacy is and how to set boundaries. It also teaches them that it is all right for them to set boundaries for being alone in the bathroom.

47. At what age do you remember bathing yourself? _____

48. At what age were you no longer allowed to enter the bathroom while a parent was bathing? _____

49. At what age do you remember asking for privacy from parents and siblings during personal bathing time?

_____

50. Enemas are an indirect form of sexual abuse and can produce feelings of invasion, powerlessness and shame. Enemas also can damage boundaries.

A sense of overwhelming powerlessness sets us up to have issues in adulthood around self-protection and care in interpersonal experiences and in sexual situations.

Did you ever receive enemas? _____
If so, how do you remember feeling during such an experience or experiences? _____

_____

51. Did you ever have a medical condition that involved manipulation of your genital area for medical examination or for the purposes of applying medication? _____ If so, describe the incident: _____

_____

Describe how you felt about this:

_____

Excessive genital infections or rashes can be a symptom of childhood sexual trauma. Medical procedures involving the genital areas during childhood are forms of indirect sexual abuse, even if they are necessary. These experiences produce feelings of shame, humiliation and powerlessness.

52. If you have had experiences similar to those described in questions 50 or 51, please describe how these experiences are still affecting you now (fearful of doctors, bladder or urethral infections, sexual difficulties):

_____

53. In adulthood how do your parents behave regarding boundaries when they are using the toilet or bathroom for bathing or changing? _____

_____

54. In adulthood how do your parents behave regarding boundaries when you are using the toilet, changing clothes or bathing? _____

_____

55. In adulthood how do you behave regarding boundaries when you are using the toilet, changing clothes or bathing? _____

_____

56. If you have children, how do you be-
    have regarding boundaries when
    they are using the toilet, changing
    clothes or bathing? _____

_____

SEX

Our first concepts of sex are developed
within our family of origin. Sexual abuse
and lack of healthy sexual information affect
our sexual boundaries. Our parents' inappropriate sexual acting-out, intimacy problems, sexual dysfunction and unresolved
childhood sexual trauma can greatly affect
our sexual boundaries. As adults we can find
ourselves with intimacy problems or sexual
dysfunction. We can even discover that we
are sexually addicted, love addicted or in (or
previously in) a severely dysfunctional relationship with an addicted individual.

One of the first questions I ask a new
client is, "How was sex discussed in your
family of origin?" or "Who told you about
sex?" These loaded questions can provide
immediate information about the boundaries
we grew up with. So many of us have been

indirectly sexually abused as a result of our parents' faulty sexual boundaries. Indirect sexual abuse is unintentional. Even so, it can set us up in adulthood to be confused about sexual matters and to lack clarity about our own sexual boundaries.

Exploring our own sexual history can provide a great deal of information about our current behavior that is causing difficulty, confusion and even pain. Some of us will begin to see parallels between our adult sexuality and our first experiences with the topic of sex in our family of origin.

57. Who told you about sex? _____ How was it presented to you by your parents? Were you satisfied with this presentation? _____ If not why? _____

_____

58. How did your parents discuss sex in general with one another, with siblings or in regarding pregnancy before marriage, premarital sex, birth control, abortion, inter-racial marriage, homosexuality and so on? _____

_____

Did they believe the above were sinful? _____

59. Did your parents have specific attitudes toward women who had sex before marriage? _____ If so, what were they? _____

_____

What was their attitude toward men who had sex before marriage? _____

_____

60. Were there restrictions around style of dress for you as an adolescent? (Example: no short skirts or makeup for girls; no long hair or tight pants for boys): _____ Was dating controlled? (Example: not allowed to date certain people from particular social backgrounds or ethnic groups):

_____

61. How old were you at the time of your first sexual experience? _____ Describe your experience: _____

_____

How many sexual partners have you had in your lifetime? _____ Do you ever use sex to feel validated, worth-

while or to change the way you feel?
_____ If so, describe instances of this:

_____

_____

_____

62. Do you like sex? _____ Do you feel
like your sexual appetite is unusually
excessive or less than normal? _____
Have you ever been accused of being
too sexual or frigid? _____ Do you
have concerns about any of your
sexual behavior? _____ If so, what
concerns you? _____
Have you ever discussed this with a
friend or a helping professional?
_____ If not, it is suggested you find
a therapist to talk to.

63. How did your parents feel about
masturbation? _____ Who did talk
to you about masturbating? _____
Describe the conversation: _____

_____

Some children were punished for
masturbating. If this happened to
you, describe the experience: _____

_____

Carla Wills-Brandon

Do you masturbate today? ＿＿＿ Do
you feel it is excessive or too limit-
ed? ＿＿＿ Do you use masturbation
in place of your sexual relationship
with your spouse or lover to relieve
painful feelings or when bored?
＿＿＿ If so, you may be using sex
addictively. If you do not masturbate
at all, how do you feel about this?

_____

64. If you are homosexual did you tell
    your family? ＿＿＿ If so, how does
    your family feel about your sexual
    preference? _____
    Describe how they reacted when
    you first shared your sexual prefer-
    ence with them: _____

    _____

    How did your father react? ＿＿＿

    _____

    How did your mother react? ＿＿＿

    _____

    How did your siblings react? ＿＿＿

    _____

    Did you feel accepted or rejected, or
    is there just a "no talk" rule about

your sexuality? _____ Do you feel completely comfortable with your sexuality? Do you have shame, excessive fear of what others say or confusion about your sexuality? _____ If you do, I suggest you speak to a therapist who understands gay issues. If we are not comfortable with our sexuality, we have difficulty understanding boundaries.

65. If you are not gay, have you ever wondered at one time or another if you possibly were? _____ If the concern was during adulthood, this can be related to unresolved sexual abuse issues. Usually it is in response to being sexually abused by the same sex. Same-sex abuse, as with opposite-sex abuse, causes a great deal of boundary blurring. Sexual abuse, direct or indirect, can create a great deal of confusion around personal sexuality.

Are either of your parents homosexual or bisexual, or have you ever suspected that either of them had

gender issues? _____ If our parents'
sexuality is a secret, this can affect
our own concept of our sexuality. If
your parents are heterosexual, do
either of them appear to have difficulty appreciating their own sex?
(Example: Mom doesn't know how
to love herself as a woman; has few
women friends; is cold, distant and
at times overly critical of other females, including her daughters. Dad
has difficulty appreciating his male-
ness, is withdrawn and distant, has
few close male friends, has homo-
phobic tendencies and has difficulty
expressing his feelings.) _____
_____

If the above is true, describe your
parents' behavior with regard to
these issues: _____
_____

How have these issues affected you
and your perception of yourself?
_____

Do you find yourself consciously
working at not being like one or both
of your parents? _____ If so, what

characteristics of theirs do you fear developing? _____
When our parents have difficulty appreciating themselves and caring for their well-being in healthy ways, this is an indication of their own un-resolved abuse issues from child-hood. Are you aware if either of your parents have abuse issues? _____ If so, describe them: _____

_____

When our parents do not own their own abuse issues, this is a form of indirect abuse for us, and it can greatly impact our boundaries.

66. Can you say no to sexual advances of another if you are not in the mood for sex, or do you engage in sexual encounters when you really don't want to? _____ If you said yes, how do you feel about this? _ _____

_____

Cite a recent example of such be-havior: _____

_____

If you are single, how soon after an

initial meeting with another in a dating situation do you find yourself
engaging in a sexual relationship?

_____

If you are married or in a significant
relationship, have you ever found
yourself engaging in sexual acts you
find distasteful? _____ Describe a
recent incident: _____

_____

BASIC BOUNDARY BEHAVIOR

"What about the word no is it you do not understand, Carla?" This was a phrase I heard from several close friends who had the courage to confront my inability to use this word. Many of us, when asked to do something by another person, have *no* on the tips of our tongues only to hear ourselves replying *yes.* As we listen to ourselves say yes to the requests of others over and over again when we do not want to, we kick ourselves and follow through resentfully with our commitment.

The ability to say no is acquired between the ages of eighteen months and three years. The following questions will help you sort out where your concepts of this word originated.

    67. Check any of the items below that you have difficulty saying no to:

          _____ Requests for your services (making cakes for a family gathering, fixing a relative's car, giving a friend a ride, babysitting a relative's or friend's child when you don't want to)

_____ Requests from others to borrow your personal belongings when you don't want to lend them

_____ Requests from others to borrow money from you when you do not have extra money or don't feel like lending it

_____ Invitations to events or gatherings you find boring

_____ Sexual advances from spouse, lover or dating partner when you are not in the mood

_____ Requests to participate in sexual activities that feel emotionally or physically uncomfortable or seem distasteful to you

_____ Touches, hugs or kisses offered by others when you would rather not

_____ Gifts received from others, which you feel uncomfortable taking

_____ Offers of food or drink when you are not hungry or thirsty

_____ Requests from others to listen to them, even when you are not in the mood or have something you need to be doing instead

_____ Phone calls from others when you are busy or engaged in an activity important to you

_____ Relatives who invite themselves over to your home without asking

_____ Friends who invite themselves over to your home without asking

_____ Relatives who invite themselves over to your home for an overnight stay

_____ Friends who invite themselves for an overnight stay

68. If you have a spouse or lover, are you able to say no to his or her requests when you do not want to fulfill them? _____

69. If you answered no, describe those requests you have difficulty saying no to: _____

_____

70. Do you ever say no to a request from a significant other, then find yourself fulfilling it anyway? _____

_____

_____

71. If you answered yes, describe these experiences: _____

_____

_____

72. If you have children, are you able to say no to your children's requests when you feel they are not appropriate? _____

73. Do you feel you have to explain your decision? _____

74. Do you ever say no to your children only to give in later? _____

75. If you answered yes, describe some instances of this behavior: _____

_____

76. Have you ever been told you are a pushover, too easy or been accused of spoiling your kids? _____

77. How do you feel about your parenting skills and ability to set healthy limits with your children? _____

_____

_____

78. Have you ever been accused of being too rigid, too strict or too controlling with your children? _____

79. If so, describe times when this has happened: _____

_____

_____

Most of us parent one of two ways: with little or no boundaries at all, or with rigid uncompromising rules. Both are in the extreme and dysfunctional. Both are a product of our own upbringing and a result of the reactions to the word no.

80. Do you remember saying no to your parents while growing up? _____ Think back in your childhood and remember how your mother responded to you when you said no. Describe what happened: _____
_____
_____

81. Describe what happened when you said no to your father: _____
_____
_____

82. Some children are punished for saying no to their parents. If you were punished, you were discouraged from setting boundaries. If you were punished with emotional withdrawal, ignoring behavior, physical hitting or verbal reprimand, describe these abuses: _____
_____

83. How did you feel about these incidents then? _____
_____

84. How do you feel about them now?
_____
_____

85. Are you fearful of rejection, abandonment or punishment for saying no to friends and relatives today as an adult? _____

86. If so, can you relate these fears to any childhood experiences? _____ If so, describe them and how they are related to today's experiences: _____
_____
_____

87. We also learn how to use the word no by watching our parents. The adult women in my family of origin had great difficulty using the word no and I rarely remember hearing any of them use it. As a consequence it never occurred to me to refuse the requests of others. I truly believed I did not have a choice and that, if asked, my only option was to follow through and comply.
Do you feel your mother had difficulty saying no to the requests of your father, relatives, neighbors, co-workers, yourself or your siblings? _____ If so, describe instances of

this: _____
_____
_____

88. Did your father have difficulty saying no to your mother, his in-laws, his parents, friends, neighbors, you or your siblings? _____ If so, describe instances of this: _____
_____
_____

89. Sometimes it was easier for my parents to say no to the neighbors or co-workers, but more difficult with family members. Were there particular people either of your parents had difficulty saying no to? _____

90. As adults we find it is easier to say no to certain people. List those people you have difficulty saying no to (relatives, friends, co-workers): _____
_____
_____

91. Do any of the people you listed above have similar physical characteristics, common behavioral patterns or other things in common?

(For example, I had difficulty with
men who had strong personalities
and who were loud. I found it difficult to say no to such individuals because they were intimidating.) _____

_____

92. When someone is behaving in a particular way (like a victim, a tyrant or
a whiner), do you find it more difficult to say no to their requests?
_____ If yes, describe this: _____

93. With the information gathered from
questions 90, 91 and 92, examine
what it is you need to do in order to
be able to say no to others. You
might need to do family of origin
work, assertiveness training or
anger work with a therapist to reclaim your power. When I was
around the people who had abused
me in my youth or when I was in the
company of people with characteristics similar to those who abused me,
I lost my power to say no. I had to
work through my own abuse issues

to learn how to feel my own power
and say no when necessary, regard-
less of the personality.

List your plan of action for learning
how to say no:

• I will _____
• I will _____
• I will _____

94. Are you committed to following
through on this plan? _____ If so,
congratulations! You are beginning
to reclaim yourself! It is most important for us to learn that when
we say no to others in order to take
care of ourselves, we are not being
selfish, self-centered or ungrateful.
We are being adults who are aware
that we are responsible for our own
well-being and that it is our job to
take care of ourselves.

EMOTIONAL INCEST

Many of us grew up in families that were filled with emotional incest. Unfortunately many of us had relationships with adults during childhood that placed us in the roles of "Daddy's Little Princess," "Mama's Little Man," "Father's Caretaker" or "Mother's Protector." These roles set us up to take care of others in adulthood. Many of us, as a result of the emotional incest in our families of origin, are still emotionally taking care of one or more of our relatives today.

Let's look at JoAnne's story: JoAnne and her father had a special relationship. When JoAnne's father came home from work, he and JoAnne would go into the backyard to talk. At these times JoAnne's father would always have a small gift of chocolate or a toy for her and he would share with her his day at the office. JoAnne loved the attention she received, even though she did not understand half of what her father was talking about. All that office stuff was very confusing, but she gave her father delighted attention anyway.

When JoAnne went away to college, her father would call to share with her what his life was like. JoAnne would become irritated with her father's lack of interest in her own life. She would pretend to listen while cleaning her dorm room or while watching television, relieved at the end of the conversation.

When JoAnne married, she was still receiving phone calls several times a week from her father. Busy with her two children and husband, she resented her father's need for her time, but knew she could never say anything for she was the only person he had to share with. She hated taking care of her father emotionally in this way and would find herself taking her frustrations out on her children or husband by raging after phone calls from her father. At times she would accuse her husband of demanding too much of her time, just as her father did. JoAnne felt confused and overwhelmed. She was full of fear the day her mother died because she knew that now her father would be even more needy.

95. Did you have a special relationship with a parent, grandparent or other adult during your childhood? _____ If so, who was this adult? _____ Describe the relationship: _____

_____

_____

96. Did this relationship make you feel more grown-up? _____ Did this relationship make you behave in a more grown-up manner? _____ If so, how? _____

_____

If you answered yes to questions 95 and 96 you have been indirectly abused. This type of abuse is called *emotional incest* and it can produce damaged boundaries in childhood. Carried into adulthood these damaged boundaries create severe intimacy problems in relationships. This type of behavior is usually not seen as abusive, but it is. The child involved is forced to grow up too quickly in order to meet the emotional needs of an adult. Emotional incest breeds co-dependent behavior along with an overwhelming need to be needed.

HAVE YOU BEEN OVEREMPOWERED?

With emotional incest comes the feeling of *overempowerment.* The overempowered child believes the world rotates around him or her and many grow up with an insatiable need for attention. Others find they have difficulty understanding simple concepts like sharing, asking for help and working with others.

Difficulties within relationships are numerous. Most overempowered children receive strokes for parental caretaking and feel wanted, needed and important. The fear of not being noticed, important and abandoned perpetuates the behavior. This behavior continues in adulthood for many of us, and a number of us are still caretaking a parent or relative today at the expense of ourselves, our husbands, wives or lovers and even our children. The overempowered child who caretakes loses the gift of childhood, which is gone before it can ever be fully experienced.

97. For those overempowered with emotionally incestuous relationships, it is often difficult to see how we have been abused. The following

are characteristics of an overempowered individual. Check those that apply to you.

_____ You have difficulty expressing anger, sadness or loneliness.

_____ You have a deep sense of loneliness.

_____ You are usually self-sufficient ("I'll just do it myself").

_____ You have difficulty in asking for help.

_____ You have a strong need to appear in control to others.

_____ You have a strong need for perfection.

_____ You are in a caretaking career.

_____ You are fearful of intimacy or opening up honestly to others.

_____ You have difficulty communicating in healthy ways with the same sex.

_____ You do a lot of listening in relationships and have difficulty

getting your own emotional
needs met.

_____ You get "dumped on" with
other people's problems.

_____ You feel obligated to be available for one or both parents,
siblings and so on whenever
needed; or you play parent or
sibling counselor or caretaker
on a regular basis at the expense of self, current spouse
or relationship or children.

_____ You have difficulty setting
limits with parental or sibling
requests; you have difficulty
saying no to relatives.

_____ Your spouse or relationship
partner has complained about
the demands of in-laws or
other relatives.

_____ You defend your family's behavior to your partner.

_____ You sometimes feel grandiose
or so powerful that you could
change history all by yourself;

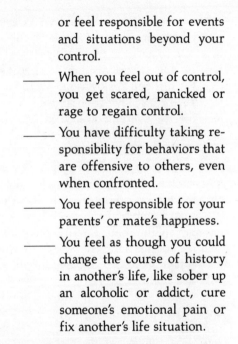

or feel responsible for events and situations beyond your control.

_____ When you feel out of control, you get scared, panicked or rage to regain control.

_____ You have difficulty taking responsibility for behaviors that are offensive to others, even when confronted.

_____ You feel responsible for your parents' or mate's happiness.

_____ You feel as though you could change the course of history in another's life, like sober up an alcoholic or addict, cure someone's emotional pain or fix another's life situation.

Overempowered individuals tend to be over-controlling and over-responsible. They tend to be attracted to people they can fix and rescue because in childhood they were set up to take care of others emotionally and even physically.

Most overempowered children have experienced emotional incest and been set up to meet the needs of one or both parents. This type of abuse is usually indirect. Because of this it is difficult for overempowered adults to realize they have been abused. It is impossible for overempowered individuals to have healthy boundaries and successful relationships until they learn how to set boundaries with their family of origin. For some this involves emotionally divorcing the parent who has set up the emotionally incestuous relationship and re-establishing a relationship with that parent consisting of healthy boundaries. The word no will be used when necessary and appropriate. Benefits are realized by resolving those issues of overempowerment originating in childhood. As our relationships with members of our family of origin improve, our relationships with others greatly improve as well.

98. If you have been abused by a special relationship with an adult in childhood or as a consequence of overempowerment, describe it: _____

_____

99. Describe how the above continues to affect you in your relationships today: _____

_____

100. List what you need to do to resolve your overempowered behavior (therapy, treatment, family of origin workshops, 12-Step meetings such as Co-dependence Anonymous, Al-Anon, Adult Children of Alcoholics):

_____

_____

_____

101. If you have made a decision to explore your history as an overempowered child, I really congratulate you. This is one of the most difficult family of origin issues to explore because as a child you got a payoff — special attention. Even though it felt good at times, many of us have paid a big price for those strokes and continue to do so in adulthood. What is your payoff today (feeling powerful, receiving attention, feeling special)?

_____

Congratulations on your honesty!

FEAR OF ABANDONMENT

Another feeling that sets us up to have difficulty setting boundaries in adulthood is an overwhelming fear of abandonment. Usually this feeling has its origins in our youth and is in response to some unresolved trauma. Whenever children are emotionally, physically or sexually abused, they are also being abandoned, as their well-being is being totally ignored. In adulthood some of us allowed ourselves to be abused by others and do not confront such behavior for fear of being abandoned. It seems to be easier for us to accept the abuse than to experience possible abandonment by confronting such behavior. The following questions will help you determine if your own fears of abandonment interfere with your ability to set limits with others.

102. Think about the times you have given in to the requests of others when you did not want to. At any of these

times were you fearful of saying no
because you were afraid they would
not like you? _____ If so, describe
some of these situations: _____

_____

103. Have you ever accepted hostile, dis-
counting or shaming remarks from
another and not defended yourself
for fear they would end the relationship or leave you? If so, describe
this: _____

_____

104. Have you ever wanted to confront
someone on behavior that was offensive to you but did not because
you were fearful of their reactions? _____ If yes, what reaction
were you afraid of? _____

105. Are you fearful of confronting your
parents, siblings or relatives about
their behaviors because you fear being ignored, abandoned, rejected,
raged at or shamed? _____ If yes,
describe how each of the following
would react if you confronted them,

said no to them or set limits on their behavior or demands:

- Mother: _____
- Father: _____
- Brother: _____
- Sister: _____
- Grandparent: _____
- Grandparent: _____
- Aunt: _____
- Uncle: _____
- Others: _____

106. Are you fearful of confronting your mate, children, friends or co-workers for fear of being ignored, abandoned, rejected, raged at or shamed? _____ If yes, describe how the following people would react to your setting boundaries with them or confronting them:

- Spouse, lover: _____
- Child: _____
- Child: _____

- Friend: _____
- Friend: _____
- Co-worker: _____
- Boss: _____

107. Do you see any similarities between 105 and 106? _____ If yes, what are they? _____
_____
_____

108. Are you fearful of being alone? _____ If so, what scares you the most about being alone? _____

109. Do you ever feel God has abandoned you or that there really isn't a God? _____ This is a typical reaction to childhood abandonment. I have not met one atheist yet who didn't have severe abandonment issues in childhood.

110. Do you abandon yourself, your desires, wishes and goals to be available to others so that they will not leave you? _____ In order to learn

how to set boundaries with others, we must first learn how to not abandon ourselves.

111. Many of us abandon our emotional, physical, sexual and spiritual needs to be available to others in fear of being abandoned. As a consequence of this, we do not set boundaries with others. How do you see that you abandon yourself in order to take care of others? List three ways you do this:

- _____
- _____
- _____

112. Where do you believe your fear of abandonment originated? _____
_____
_____

113. How do you see the above influencing your life today? _____
_____

114. What do you need to do to stop abandoning yourself? _____

_____

_____

115. Some of us are so fearful of abandonment, we need outside assistance, such as therapy, to work through these issues. If you are in need of outside assistance, what are you willing to do? _____

_____

116. When will you do the above? _____
You have just contracted with yourself to resolve your abandonment fears. I wish you well on your journey!

TRIANGULATION

117. Triangulation interferes with our ability to set boundaries with family members and others. As the "go-between" for two other people, our boundaries are blurred and often nonexistent. We feel confused in this situation. Look at the following diagrams and plot the triangles in which you were involved.

Carla Wills-Brandon

Figure 1. Unhealthy Communication

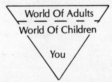

Figure 2. Healthy Communication

118. How do you feel when involved in triangles (mad, glad, sad, empowered, special, needed)? _____

119. If you have been involved in triangles, describe your role (the go-between, the message-sender or the message-receiver): _____

120. Have you ever found yourself in trouble or in sticky situations as a

consequence of being involved in a
triangle? _____

121. Do you ever remember your parents
using you as a "go-between" for
them? For example: "Tell your mother I'm angry with her." "Tell your
father to pick up the laundry." "Tell
your father I'm not going out to-
night. I have a cold." "Tell your
mother to go to the doctor." "Tell
your father to get a new suit." If so,
describe the types of messages you
heard.

- _____
- _____
- _____

122. Do you ever find yourself listening
to one of your parents complain
about the other or about another relative or friend? _____ If so, do you
find yourself ever giving advice?
_____ Have you ever found yourself
in an uncomfortable situation because of your advice-giving? _____

Or from getting involved with the problems of another's relationship? _____ If so, describe this: _____

_____

123. We learn triangulation in childhood. It gives us a sense of power to be included and involved in the lives of others, but sometimes our involvement can backfire with both parties angry with us. Triangulation can become emotionally exhausting and frustrating. Some of us fear being left out of the action and involve ourselves in triangulation from the fear of being abandoned. Describe examples listed above that have happened in your life: _____

_____

124. What is your payoff for being involved in triangles? _____

_____

Is it worth it? _____ If not, how come? _____

_____

125. To avoid triangulation, you can:

- Tell the other person you care about them but do not wish to get in the middle of their relationship problems.
- Tell the other person that if they have something to say to someone else, they probably need to share it with them instead of you.
- Tell them that you don't feel comfortable delivering messages for them.
- Tell them if they want to know how your friend is doing, they might want to call him or her.
- Tell them if they are angry with the other person, they need to tell them.
- Tell them you care for both of them and do not wish to take sides.
- Tell them you have got yourself into trouble by being in the middle before and choose not to do this again.

It is also important for us to be aware of when we are setting up others to carry our messages. (The last time I tried to set up one of my sisters to carry a message to the other during a phone conversation, she threatened to hang up the phone. I was so used to being

involved in triangles that I found myself un-
consciously passing information on to my other sister. I was amazed at how natural this
felt and had to examine why I did not want
to relay my message myself.) Many times we
feel safer having our messages relayed for
us, fearing the reaction of the receiver. If this
is the case, we need to examine why.

If there have been instances in your life of
triangulation, list one and say what you could
have told the person in order to stop the
triangulation: _____
_____

126. If you have set up another person to
pass messages in triangles, take a
look at why it has not felt safe for
you to be direct. What were your
fears? _____
_____

127. In order for us to develop healthy
boundaries, it is important for us not
to participate in triangulation. For
the next week observe triangles in
which you are involved. Examine
them by drawing diagrams and brief-

ly describe the situations and participants.

128. What did you discover? _____
_____
_____

129. What role are you usually in (sender,
messenger, receiver)? _____

130. How do you feel about participation
in triangles now? _____

131. Is the payoff for your participation
worth it? _____

132. What are your fears about pulling
out of the triangles in which you are
involved? _____
_____

133. It is important to address these behaviors in order to begin establishing
healthy boundaries. Triangulation
stunts honesty, true intimacy and
healthy conflict resolution. What do
you feel is necessary for you to do to
begin addressing your participation
in triangles? (Examine family of origin for source of behavior, contract
with self to not triangulate, seek

therapy.): _____

_____

134. It is difficult to avoid triangulation, and in many situations others are not too pleased with us when we stop our participation. Triangulation is also a form of caretaking. (As long as my sister was carrying messages from me to my other sister, she was caretaking by not holding me responsible for delivering my own messages. When she first set a boundary and said no to my request, I was angry with her for not taking care of me. "How dare she!" I thought, until I realized my request was violating her boundaries.) If you were stopped when you were attempting to triangulate, how did you feel?

_____

_____

DEALING WITH ANGER

In many situations our fears of setting boundaries or saying no are about our fears of the reactions of others. A number of us have difficulty with another being angry with us. Some of us even freeze when confronted with the anger of another. This response usually has its source in our family of origin and is a consequence of our parents' behavior surrounding the emotion of anger. Fearing the angry responses of others can set the stage for dysfunctional boundaries. Let's take a look at how our family of origin dealt with anger by completing questions 135 through 155:

135. When my father was angry, he _____
___ _____

136. I knew my father was angry when
_____
_____

137. I feared my father's anger because
_____
_____

138. When my father was angry with me, he would _____
_____

139. The most angry I ever saw my father was _____

140. He behaved in the following ways _____
_____

141. During this time I felt _____

142. When my mother was angry, she _____
_____

143. I knew my mother was angry when _____
_____

144. I feared my mother's anger because _____
_____

145. When my mother was angry with me, she would _____
_____

146. The most angry I ever saw my mother was when _____
_____

147. During this time I felt _____
_____

148. When I am confronted by an angry
person, I react by _____
_____

149. When I am angry, I _____
_____

150. When I am confronted by an angry
person, I feel _____
_____

151. When I am angry at others, their responses have been _____
_____

152. When I tell my father I am angry
with him, he _____
_____
_____

153. When I tell my mother I am angry
with her, she _____
_____

154. How are your mother's and father's
behavior with anger during your
childhood still affecting you today in
your relationships and in your ability

to set healthy boundaries? List three consequences.

- _____
- _____
- _____

155. Most of us fear our own anger and stuff it, never allowing it to surface. Many of us explore and rage, offending those around us. How do you express your anger? _____
_____
_____

Healthy expression of anger involves owning it, admitting it and working through it as it surfaces. Most of us do not know that the following phrases are not only healthy but healing:

- "I'm angry with you because . . ."
- "I'm angry that didn't go the way I thought it would."
- "I'm angry with my spouse, children, parents, boss because . . ."
- "I'm angry you're not there for me."
- "I'm angry I've abandoned myself."

- "I'm angry I don't know how to set boundaries with you."
- "I'm angry that you violated my boundaries."
- "I'm angry you expect me to fix you."
- "I'm angry that you are triangulating."

Stuffing our anger until we rage or get sick emotionally or physically is a display of unhealthy boundaries. Beginning to experience our own anger as it surfaces requires dealing with our anger in healthy ways. Examples of healthy expression of anger include: talking about it, doing rage work in therapy, discussing it in a 12-Step meeting, writing about it, sharing it with the person we are angry at or by hitting a stack of pillows with a plastic baseball bat.

When we can have our own anger in healthy ways, we slowly learn that another's anger will not kill us. I always thought the anger of others would destroy me and did whatever it took with people-pleasing behavior to avoid this. Today it is not uncommon at one time or another for my husband, child, relatives, friends, co-workers or peers to be angry with me for my behavior (appropriate or inappropriate) or when I set boundaries. Being angry with one another is not only normal but healthy.

When we express our anger toward one another, we are building healthy boundaries. Intimacy is promoted by saying "I care about you enough to be honest and say . . ." "I care about our relationship enough to share how dissatisfied I am with . . ." Learning how to confront the bogeyman — anger — begins by examining what we learned about anger in our family of origin. We can then decide whether what we learned was healthy and choose to hang on to those beliefs or let go and develop our own.

Healthy anger allows us to take care of ourselves and it allows others to do the same. When we decide to begin to establish healthy boundaries, we are bound to experience anger from those who have difficulty with our new way of living.

To believe that all those around us will be happy with our new way of being is unrealistic. I thought everyone would be pleased as punch that I was giving up my membership card to "Victims Anonymous" and taking care of myself in healthy responsible ways. I was way off base! I began to realize that as in all things in life, there are consequences to change. Some of the consequences of my new boundaries were not only surprising, but unexpected and confusing.

Some were as happy as could be upon learning I now had the tools to take care of myself in healthy, adult ways. When I set limits with these individuals, their responses were supportive and understanding. Others responded with surprise, hurt feelings and often anger when I would say no, stand up for myself, have an opinion or care for myself with other healthy limit-setting behaviors. They said, "If you really cared, you would say yes!" "Isn't that awfully selfish of you?" "I thought you were my friend — what do you mean I can't borrow . . . ?" Or "Carla, you used to be so agreeable! What has happened to you?" and "Carla, you really are arrogant if you think I was trying to use you for . . . !" and so on.

At first my feelings were really hurt. I also felt very confused. Fortunately about half of these individuals eventually agreed that I did need to set boundaries and not behave like such a doormat. They too were weary of my victim behavior. They began to affirm my right to set boundaries and apologized for their lack of support. They acknowledged that my new behavior produced change in our relationship. As a result of this I was able to establish new lines of communication with these individuals and enjoy healthy intimacy for the first time in these relationships. As for the other half, unfortunately, most are to this day still angry with me for saying:

- No, I don't think so.
- I disagree.
- That's unacceptable to me.
- I agree to disagree.
- I'm feeling used.
- I don't feel like being hugged right now.
- I'm sorry, but I can't listen right now.
- I will not allow myself to be abused.
- What you are saying to me feels abusive and I'm leaving.
- No, I have other plans.
- Please don't do that because it hurts.

These individuals, I sadly realized, were not willing to accept my new behavior. They would continue to accept me only if I did not have boundaries. By taking care of myself I was unavailable to take care of them as I had so often in the past. They viewed my behavior as unacceptable and in several cases they became offensive. I was raged at, shamed and accused of being inappropriate for saying no.

I felt a deep sense of sadness when I realized that not everyone was going to support me in my new behavior. I had to have my anger and grieve these relationships in order to let them go. I recognized that I could not go back to old behavior to hang on to these individuals.

I discovered that my new boundaries had given me something I had never had before: the gift of a strong sense of self-respect. My new-found self-respect produced an incredible sensation of self-love that started at the tip of my toes and ran warmly through my entire being. I realized I no longer needed to dysfunctionally give in order to be accepted by others. I now had the ability to accept myself. Nor did I have to isolate in pain from others for fear of being used and abused. For the first time in my life I loved myself just enough to know

I was worth protecting and caring about, no matter who else was involved.

Today not everybody likes me. With those friendships I do enjoy, there is a healthy sense of respect that runs both ways and an equal amount of taking and giving. It is acceptable to state not only one's boundaries, but one's needs as well.

What is most important today is that *I like me.* This allows me the experience of enjoying others in healthy ways. In order to learn about loving others in healthy ways, we must first begin with ourselves. When we can truly love ourselves, we begin to experience healthy relationships with others. When we love ourselves we can experience our relationship with our planet. With this love we begin to create for ourselves the greatest gift of all: the gift of healthy spirituality. We become active participants in the wonderful experience of life.

Healthy boundary building is one of the most difficult tasks we ever have to tackle in our lives because it means we are accepting total responsibility for ourselves. Initially this can feel pretty scary. Most of us have never really known how to do this. We have either taken care of others or isolated ourselves from the world in fear. Healthy boundaries free us not only to explore this wonderful world in which we live, but at the same time to know, deep in our hearts that we can be safe and take care of ourselves. We can take care of ourselves and be safe no matter what life dishes out for us. This makes our journey through this experience called life an adventure as opposed to a struggle. Today we can all be an active part of life instead of feeling lost in it.

Good luck to you on your journey. Know that you are already on the right path!

Other Books By Carla Wills-Brandon

Eat Like A Lady:
Guide For Overcoming Bulimia
ISBN 1-55874-008-2　　　　　　　$7.95

Is It Love Or Is It Sex?
Why Relationships Don't Work
ISBN 1-55874-027-9　　　　　　　$8.95

Learning To Say No
Establishing Healthy Boundaries
ISBN 1-55874-087-6　　　　　　　$8.95

Health Communications, Inc.
3201 S.W. 15th Street
Deerfield Beach, FL 33442-8190
Phone: (800) 851-9100

Resources

—

Al-Anon, Al-Anon
Adult Children of
Alcoholics and Alateen
Family Groups
P.O. Box 862
Midtown Station
New York, NY
10018-086

Alcoholics Anonymous
Box 459
Grand Central Station
New York, NY 10163

Adult Children of
Alcoholics
6381 Hollywood Blvd.
Suite 685
Hollywood, CA 90028

Cocaine Anonymous
P.O. Box 1367
Culver City, CA 90232

Nar-Anon
P.O. Box 2562
Palo Verdes, CA 90274

Pill-Anon Famiy
Programs
P.O. Box 120
Gracie Station
New York, NY
10028

Co-dependents
Anonymous —
Central Office
P.O. Box 5508
Glendale, AZ 85312

National Association
for Adult Children
of Alcoholics
31582 Coast Highway
Suite B
Laguna Beach, CA
92677

Parents Without
Partners
7910 Woodmont Ave.
Washington, DC
20014

Family Violence
Batterers Anonymous
P.O. Box 29
Redlands, CA 92373

Survivors Network
18653 Ventura Blvd.
#143
Tarzana, CA 91356

Eating Disorders
Overeaters
Anonymous
4025 Spenser Street
Suite 203
Torrance, CA 90503

Food Addicts
Anonymous
P.O. Box 057394
West Palm Beach, FL
33405

Sexual Disorders
Sexual Addicts
Anonymous
P.O. Box 3038
Minneapolis, MN
55403

CoSA (Co-dependent
of Sexual Addicts)
Twin Cities CoSA
P.O. Box 14357
Minneapolis, MN
55414

Incest
Incest Survivors
Anonymous
P.O. Box 5613
Long Beach, CA
90805

Sexual Abuse
Anonymous
P.O. Box 80085
Minneapolis, MN
55408